A PROPERTY SOURCING BUSINESS

The moral right of the author has been asserted.

Apart from any fair dealing for the purposes of research or private study, or criticism or review, as permitted under the Copyright, Designs and Patents Act 1988, this publication may only be reproduced, stored or transmitted, in any form or by any means, with the prior permission in writing of the publishers, or in the case of reprographic reproduction in accordance with the terms of licences issued by the Copyright Licensing Agency. Enquiries concerning reproduction outside those terms should be sent to the publishers.

Matador
9 Priory Business Park,
Wistow Road, Kibworth Beauchamp,
Leicestershire. LE8 0RX
Tel: (+44) 116 279 2299
Fax: (+44) 116 279 2277
Email: books@troubador.co.uk
Web: www.troubador.co.uk/matador

ISBN 978 1783064 960

British Library Cataloguing in Publication Data.
A catalogue record for this book is available from the British Library.

Typeset by Troubador Publishing Ltd, Leicester, UK
Printed and bound in the UK by TJ International, Padstow, Cornwall

Matador is an imprint of Troubador Publishing Ltd

BRICK BUY BRICK A PROPERTY SOURCING BUSINESS

INTRODUCTION

This book, in the Brick Buy Brick educational series focusing on creating a property sourcing business, has been written in association with Tigrent Learning UK, the UK's most respected provider of professional training programmes.

Tigrent and its associated network of industry experts and partners have a wealth of property investing knowledge. Tigrent trainers and customers derive from all ages and backgrounds and have over a decade's experience of working with new and existing investors from all over the world.

This book looks at creating a property sourcing business as a separate business unit and income stream for an investor. Some investors consider this

 A PROPERTY SOURCING BUSINESS

as a primary strategy, a way of controlling and monetising deals without having to actually purchase properties. Other investors find this a useful complimentary strategy to their investment activities that provides additional income and a diversified business base. This book will look at setting up a sourcing business, the opportunities it can offer, and how to deal with regulation to provide a professional and trustworthy service to the customers you deal with.

For more information and to give us any feedback on your reading experience please visit:

www.brick-buy-brick.co.uk.

CHAPTER ONE

A PROPERTY SOURCING BUSINESS AND SOURCING AGENTS

A property sourcing business, or operating as a sourcing agent, can be a lucrative opportunity for a property investor, either as a primary strategy or a complimentary strategy.

A sourcing business or a sourcing agent is similar to an estate agent. However, a sourcing agent works on behalf of the buyer looking for and negotiating the best property investment opportunities.

Think about traditional high street estate agents. They sell properties from a range of different

 A PROPERTY SOURCING BUSINESS

vendors that will include owner occupiers, landlords, property developers etc. The vendors selling those properties will each have individual circumstances and requirements on price, timeline and conditions for a sale of their own property. The majority of vendors selling through estate agents will be in generally strong positions or in situations where they need to sell at a price that is very much in line with the property market generally. A much smaller proportion of properties listed with estate agents will be ideal investment opportunities.

Contrasting the estate agent with the sourcing agent, the sourcing agent seeks out property deals that have an investment angle. The properties a sourcing agent presents to their investor clients might be available at a large discount, have opportunities to add substantial value through re-development or refurbishment, or may have exceptionally high yields. The sourcing agent will need to keep the purchaser's interests front and centre in assessing deals. Dealing with investment buyers, the sourcing agent will need to make sure there is a genuine money making opportunity within the deal. Think of the sourcing agent as an estate agent working for the buyer.

A sourcing agent creates value for their clients, both through property selection and also through bringing some specialised knowledge, expertise or experience to create a better investment opportunity. In property we often hear of 'fantastic investment opportunities,' and then we must move past the marketing material to assess how 'fantastic' that opportunity really is, and whether it will fit our strategy. The sourcing agent's starting point is sifting through the market to find the genuinely fantastic opportunities to present to their clients.

Your sourcing business could focus on identifying and selling opportunities for great buy to let properties, HMO's, developments, land, opportunities to flip, the list can go on and on. The key criteria is being able to assess the money making opportunity and present a strategy for realising that money making opportunity. Your own sourcing business will generally be closely aligned with your expertise and experience so that you can provide value to your clients. However, as the sourcing agent you don't need to be expert in all aspects, you might sub-contract or refer to other industry experts for certain aspects of the deal and simply provide a coordination service to your clients.

Fees for sourcing agents in many cases will exceed the levels of commission traditional estate agents charge. This is due to the specialised knowledge the sourcing agent is bringing to the investor and the sourcing agent's ability to find off-market or hard to spot opportunities. There is a lot of pricing flexibility for your sourcing business, the golden rule is to make sure there is still a genuine money making opportunity for your investor client. If you can earn a £10,000 fee while your client makes a £100,000 profit, you create a win/win situation on both sides.

As a property investor you are constantly looking at property deal leads and assessing opportunities. A property investor will also look at building a reliable power team for working through deals. A sourcing business provides an outlet to generate an income through assessing and presenting deals. Allowing your clients to tap into your tried and tested power team allows your business to generate an income from your power team's expertise.

Many investors use sourcing as a way of earning a fee from on-selling good deals that aren't the focus of their own strategy. Other investors may be in the position of beginning from a low capital base, so purchasing multiple properties or even a single property is not an option at the beginning of their investment journey. A sourcing business can also work for those investors who have issues with their credit file, meaning that lending to purchase property is not currently an option.

Sourcing is a way of controlling and earning from deals without requiring the resources to personally do the deal. Sourcing on good property deals becomes a way of not only earning from a deal that would have been passed over, but also can build

your investment pot.

As a sourcing agent you will need a strategy for finding and assessing deals. Most sourcing businesses will focus on a local area and use their expert knowledge of that area to create value. In the selected target area you will need to look at what generates the most amount of reliable property leads. As with all lead generation strategies there is an element of trial and error assessing whether you can deal with the traditional estate agents in your area, auction houses, or run direct marketing campaigns to find vendors.

 A PROPERTY SOURCING BUSINESS

CHAPTER TWO

SALES OPPORTUNITIES

Sourcing property is a multi-layered business and it's possible to earn fees at multiple levels and from multiple sources.

Unqualified Leads

Selling an unqualified lead is the base level earning opportunity for a property sourcing business. This is the simplest product you can sell, as it requires only the most basic of assessments. An unqualified lead simply is:

Property Address

 A PROPERTY SOURCING BUSINESS

Vendor Name
Vendor Contact Details

You will need to have a direct marketing strategy to generate your own leads in order to sell on these leads. No one will pay you for a lead on a property they could find themselves on one of the property marketing websites such as www.rightmove.co.uk.

Unqualified leads sell at around the £25 mark each and generally sourcing businesses offer these on a non-exclusive basis. You may be able to generate the lead and on-sell it multiple times if it is in an area of high demand for your clients.

Once you have sold on the vendor's details and the property address, as a sourcing agent your job is done, the person purchasing the lead goes on to contact and negotiate with the vendor. The business selling the unqualified lead doesn't provide any information on price or investment value – it's just an opportunity for the purchaser to get direct contact with an investor.

If you have a large scale direct marketing strategy that generates many excess leads that aren't core to your business, you may consider selling on the excess to other sourcing businesses or direct to property investors.

Qualified Leads

The next level is qualified leads. A qualified lead involves more time in assessing the opportunity, but should not involve negotiation on price or strategy setting. A qualified lead is:

Property address
Asking price or vendor's estimate of market value
Lowest price the vendor would consider selling for
Time-frame required for selling
Vendor name
Vendor contact details

As with an unqualified lead, the sourcing agent will not negotiate the deal to a conclusion. Instead, basic qualifying details regarding the property are

 A PROPERTY SOURCING BUSINESS

collected and are offered for sale. The principle is the same as an unqualified lead – the purchaser of the lead will negotiate directly with the vendor to try to strike a deal.

Qualified leads are generally priced around the £250 level, with some fluctuations up or down depending on the value of the opportunity, and whether they are offered on an exclusive basis or not.

You will require a direct marketing strategy to sell qualified leads as you will need to be able to deal direct with the seller of the property and be able to provide the seller's contact details to a third party purchaser.

Ready Made Deals / Finder's Fees

As a sourcing business you can sell ready made deals or earn a finder's fee from selling an opportunity to an experienced investor who has a team ready to execute the deal.

 A PROPERTY SOURCING BUSINESS

Imagine you are contacted by a large property developer who wants plots of land to build houses, you find land that is in the right location and of sufficient size. The developer brings his own team to deal with building the houses, and the sourcing agent would simply earn a fee for the opportunity. Bringing that back to a smaller scale, you might have a client who is a buy to let investor who is used to light refurbishment and has his own lettings team, you could sell this investor a 'ready made deal,' a property that is in a good rental location, needs some cosmetic work and is well priced. A ready made deal is:

Property Address
Asking price / Ceiling price for the style of property in the area
Negotiated price

Key requirements:
i.e. Works required, subject to current tenancy, completion in 14 days etc.
Rental value / Sales value if flipping

A ready made deal involves the sourcing agent making an assessment of the right strategy for the property and providing details on that strategy. It doesn't, however, involve the sourcing agent having to assist in executing the strategy. Selling a ready made deal or taking a finder's fee only, assumes the investor or business purchasing the deal has their own team and resources to make the deal happen.

Ready made deals are generally priced from £1,000 upwards, with complete exclusivity. Pricing will generally vary in line with the value of the deal. It is common to see fees on these types of deals presented as a similar percentage level to what you would expect from a traditional estate agent i.e. a range of 1.5% – 3% depending on the area and style of property.

Full Packaged Deals

A full packaged deal is the full service from the sourcing business. Similar to a ready made deal, in this case the sourcing business would provide

services or refer to external contractors to provide services to execute the deal.

To contrast with the ready made deal example, when selling a packaged deal your service to the buy to let investor might be:

Finding the property
Negotiating the price
Having any refurbishment or repairs costed by reputable builders
Providing a referral to a valuation company, a builder, and a lettings agent to let the property

The sourcing business would coordinate the various aspects of the deal. However, it is important to remember for skilled or professional work like valuations or building works the sourcing business should recommend or refer to qualified persons rather than trying to do everything in house.

Full packaged deals are often seen as a hands off strategy for an armchair investor. The value the sourcing business provides is that the armchair investor can have minimal involvement in the deal.

Sourcing agents generally charge upwards of £3,000 for fully packaged deals, with prices linked to the value of the property, attractiveness of the opportunity and also the level and complexity of services offered.

Case Study – Fully Packaged Deal

3 Bedroom semi-detached property in Bestwood, Nottingham

The property identified was in an area of high demand for rentals, with three bedrooms fetching between £500 and £550 per month in rent. The key requirements to achieve the higher rents in the area were good internal condition and off street parking. The property was a deceased estate, in poor cosmetic condition, requiring a lot of rubbish clearance and crucially lacked off street parking.

BRICK BUY BRICK A PROPERTY SOURCING BUSINESS

Asking price: £75,000
Purchase price: £51,000
Works Budget: £14,000
(Including all internal works, rubbish clearance and creating a parking area to the front of the property)
Fee charged by sourcing business: £5,000
Investor's legal fees: £1,000
Total outlay by investor: £71,000

Refurbishment took 7 weeks, the property was marketed for 3 weeks, and a tenant was secured at £550 per month rent on a 2 year tenancy.

The investor refinanced the property after 8 month's receiving a valuation of £90,000 and took at 75% mortgage.

The armchair investor's equity position is:

Original outlay: £71,000
Refinance funds received: £67,500
Outlay less refinance funds: £3,500
(Residual cash in the deal)

 A PROPERTY SOURCING BUSINESS

Equity Profit: £19,000

This represents an excellent opportunity for an investor who has never had to leave his home in London to visit the property. The £5,000 for finding the opportunity and coordinating a fairly simple project is also a great earning opportunity for the sourcing business.

Selling opportunities like this through a sourcing business can create a lucrative income stream.

CHAPTER THREE

FINDING DEALS

We could dedicate an entire book to strategies to locate great investment opportunities, and many investors have their own tried and tested strategies that always work for their target areas. For now, we will focus on some core general strategies.

Estate Agents

The majority of vendors, whether they are in a strong position or require a quick sale, whether they have a lovely well presented house or the type of house that you need to wipe your feet as you leave, go to traditional estate agents. Anyone serious about sourcing property deals needs to have some estate agents on speed dial. Finding deals with estate agents is all about building relationships and becoming a dependable buyer, or source of buyers, for the agent. Transaction volume with an agent will build your track record, and ensure you are offered more deals and better opportunities.

Estate agents act for the seller, and in order to maximise their sales they will want to show you as many opportunities that they can, hoping that you will bite on one. The key for the sourcing agent is to quickly filter these opportunities down to those that work as investments, then to identify which of those can be acquired at the right price. Dealing with estate agents is a game of wading through the quantity to find the quality.

Auction Houses

As a sourcing business you can identify opportunities that are going to auction, and some sourcing businesses provide a service where they will bid on their client's behalf if required. As with estate agents, it is important to remember that the auction house is acting on behalf of the vendor to sell a property, so the sourcing agent needs to critically assess the opportunities.

Auctions are a public sales forum, so sourcing property in this manner can mean that you lose some opportunities as other people are prepared to pay more on the day of the auction. However, auctions do have a higher proportion of distressed property investment opportunities or redevelopment projects so can reduce the quantity of properties you need to assess.

A tip – always make sure your investor is committed and ready to purchase before considering offering them auction property. There are strict rules at auction about time-frames for completion and stiff penalties if time-scales are not met. Many investors who do buy at auction like to know they have cash available if required to complete the purchase.

Direct to vendor marketing

Having direct access to the vendor is your best opportunity to create the best deals and also have the most control over a deal. In contrast to dealing with estate agents or auction houses, you are not at the mercy of the market; you have a one on one relationship with the vendor. You can use this close relationship to create better terms and a better deal for your investor clients, which should then maximise your fees.

There are multiple direct marketing strategies you can consider, and the key to effectively using direct marketing is to test for what works in your area, to generate the type of leads for properties that you want. You may consider:

Mass marketing:
TV, Radio or Newspaper Advertising

Outdoor marketing:
Billboards, bus shelters, sandwich boards, wrapping your car with advertising

Street level:
Leaflets, postcards, business cards

Online marketing:
Website, Facebook, Twitter, Google Ads

The decision on direct marketing comes down to two choices, budget and return.

Mass marketing is the most expensive, but hits the largest number of people, however, volume alone doesn't necessarily mean you convert leads into fees.

Outdoor marketing is a consistent presence and generally cheaper than mass media, but think carefully about footfall and how many people will see your marketing.

Street level marketing is more targeted, but it does limit your geographic coverage.

Online marketing can provide better opportunities

to target and condition leads before you speak with them, but can generate a smaller number of enquiries as the web is a cluttered place.

Split testing is a term thrown around a lot in marketing jargon, but essentially it is a simple concept whereby you compare the performance of an ad by changing one variable at a time. Try a marketing strategy, any of those noted above, however, for example purposes we'll look at a leaflet.

Step 1 – Design a leaflet, such as 'I buy houses – cash offers – any condition – my phone number'

Step 2 – Target 5 – 10 streets with houses that suit your strategy

Step 3 – Assess call volume and quality of leads – how many calls? How many quality leads?

Step 4 – Change 1 aspect at a time of your leaflet. i.e. colour, font, text, and repeat steps 2 and 3. If the

volume and quality goes up, keep the change, if it goes down, discard the change.

You can follow this same process with area. If you target a group of 5-10 streets, 2-3 times with limited volume of calls and conversions to fees, then move to the next area.

Direct marketing is very much about following a split testing formula so that you have a system to find out what works and what doesn't and repeat the process that yields the best results.

CHAPTER FOUR

DEAL STRATEGIES

As a sourcing business much of the value you charge in your fees is tied to your ability to identify a strategy for an investment property. The majority of people only see what is in front of them when they walk into a house. If the house looks beautiful, is well furnished and well cared for it will appeal. If it is run-down, messy and dirty then many people struggle to see potential. As the sourcing agent, you are always on the look out for the elusive 'potential.'

The first step is finding the deal, whether it's the worst house on the best street, or the desperate vendor who needs a speedy sale more than best

price. When you have found a property with potential you need to think about the correct strategy for that property. We will now look at some of the core strategies.

Distressed Property / Forced Appreciation

Many property investors have distressed property or forced appreciation as a core part of their strategy. As a sourcing agent, you can find properties that can be purchased below market value because the property or vendor is distressed, or you can see an opportunity for significant uplift through redevelopment or refurbishment. Properties with this opportunity provide margin in the deal, a large equity profit. The larger the equity profit, the greater the fee you can charge. This strategy can also be combined with some of the further strategies below.

Buy To Let

Buy to let essentially means buying a single residential unit to let to a single person or household. It is the simplest rental strategy for investment. Many national estate agents publish average yield figures annually as do some industry bodies. In general, buy to lets in the UK have an average yield of between 4% and 7% dependant on area and market conditions. The key to making buy to let work as an opportunity you can sell to an armchair investor, is beating the average. In order to justify your fee you need to demonstrate value to the investor by showing you can achieve at least 2-3% greater yield than the area average through careful property selection.

HMO – Houses of Multiple Occupancy

HMO is a strategy for maximising rental yield vs the floor space of the property. A property is let as a selection of rooms or bedsits with some shared facilities rather than a whole house. This strategy is popular in densely populated areas, or where there are universities or hospitals nearby and you can target students or young professionals. In some areas investors target tenants receiving local housing allowance. HMO is more specialised than buy to let. As a sourcing agent you will have to look at the property's viability to convert to HMO, additional costs, licensing requirements, and tenant demand. However, HMO can create a much higher yield for a building, maybe 14% vs 8% as a buy to let, so can provide significantly better rental return for an armchair investor, which allows you as the sourcing agent to charge a higher fee for identifying that opportunity and managing the deal.

Flipping

Flipping relies on spotting opportunities and identifying a distressed property or using a forced appreciation approach to create value. The key to the strategy is you are preparing a property for sale to the open market. As a sourcing agent, when presenting this strategy to your client base, consider the sales volume in your area and whether it is reliable and consistent. Look at the profit margin for your investor client to assess how much your fee should be for the deal.

Development / Change of Use

This is a more advanced strategy and requires more of the sourcing business in terms of time, resource and expertise. Development and change of use revolves around spotting the big opportunity for a property. Can you convert from a large house to 5 flats? Would that office building be better as a 40 bed student HMO? Could you build a mixed use retail and residential development on that car park site to make a profit? As a sourcing business if you're looking at this type of opportunity, consider whether you will deal with investors who have large proven power teams in place in return for a finder's fee, or whether you will grow your own team to include planning consultants, architects and quantity surveyors to help bring your redevelopment to life. While this is an advanced strategy, it also provides the greatest fee earning opportunity as you can maximise the value added.

When looking at the strategy for a property deal that you are presenting, consider your presentation like a business plan or investment appraisal. You

need to be able to define for your client:

1. The entry to the deal, costs, timescales etc.
2. The exit strategy/strategies
3. Any risk factors/unknowns

A good starting point for this is always to assess the deal and strategy from the point of view that you are spending your own money on it. That should mean that you provide a good level of analysis and diligence to your clients.

The importance of strategy

A property marketed with an estate agent –
Requiring modernisation and improvement, a three bedroom, two reception room terrace house with large kitchen and utility, centrally located. Would rent for up to £525 per month. Quick sale required. Asking £80,000.

What the sourcing agent sees –
A complete wreck that needs total refurbishment,

 A PROPERTY SOURCING BUSINESS

owned by a distressed vendor. Opportunity to create a 5 room HMO less than 5 minutes from town centre and less than 5 minutes from the train station. Rental potential 5 rooms x £300 per month = £1,500 per month. Better buy it quick before someone else does!

CHAPTER FIVE

FINDING CLIENTS

As a sourcing business while you need to spend your time finding deals, you also need to have a ready client base to sell those deals onto. It's important to keep both in balance to make your business function effectively.

The perfect client for a sourcing business is an armchair investor, someone who is cash rich and time poor, or who is expert in their field, which is not property, but they are interested in property and investment. You need to make sure you find clients you can deliver value to. That means finding someone who needs your skills, your expertise and your local knowledge, and who isn't capable of easily replicating it themselves.

When building your client base target people like:

Skilled workers and professionals – Those with high salaries and stable jobs are likely to have good levels of savings and be interested in investing for the long term.

Business owners – many businesses keep cash reserves which can provide an investment pot. You have the advantage, the person you are dealing with is experienced in business so can assess yield and return but may not necessarily be a property professional.

High net worth individuals – Those with large cash reserves who invest professionally for a living, they are used to looking at vehicles like property to profit.

Think about where your target investors are and mix in those circles. Consider joining networking groups, investor meetings, landlord meetings and business groups in the area. If you come from a corporate background, look at your existing network, are there people from your corporate life who might be interested in growing a property portfolio as a sideline to their current jobs? Look at strategies to meet the right type of clients, make contacts and alliances with accountants, solicitors, financial advisers and other professionals who deal with those who invest and have cash available to do so.

Your ideal client will always have a knowledge, time, or resource gap you can fill, so be ruthless about assessing whether a client is right for you. If you feel they could do it themselves, beware, you may just be giving them a shortcut to inside market knowledge of your target area.

When screening potential new clients you need to understand their financial position and motivation for purchasing investment property. A short checklist:

Do they have cash/savings to invest?

How much?

Can they obtain mortgage finance?

Can you get an agreement in principle from a lender to see how much they can borrow?

What is their risk appetite?

(Think about buy to let at one end of a scale vs development at the other)

What is their property investing experience?

As an agent negotiating to purchase property on their behalf it is reasonable you ask these questions up front and that you ask for proof to back the answers up, like bank statements, agreements in principle for finance, details of existing portfolio etc. In fact, when we deal with regulation later in the book, you'll see that you are required to collect and hold some of this information by law. By screening your clients at the start you know you have a good quality base that is ready to buy, speeding up your business's time line between finding a deal and earning a fee.

CHAPTER SIX

PRESENTING DEALS AND YOUR SERVICES

As a sourcing business your value comes from the deals and services you can provide to your clients. It's important to look at what you can offer for each deal and define this for your clients up front. This chapter is focused on those opportunities to earn larger fees at the fully packaged deal level by presenting a finished solution to your armchair investor and providing a power team who are ready to act.

In Chapter 2 we covered what you need to do to sell a fully packaged deal, now we look at how you present that to a potential client.

BRICK BUY BRICK A PROPERTY SOURCING BUSINESS

Key deal information:

How much?
Time-line
Current condition of the property
Strategy for maximising value (if required)
Rental potential
Sale potential
Your fee
Your services
Third party services

When presenting your deals include lots of photos – there is an old saying a picture is worth a thousand words – seeing potential is a lot easier than reading about potential. Consider whether you need to show examples of finished projects to illustrate the potential to your clients. If you have recently overseen a refurbishment of a buy to let property and you are presenting a similar deal, then show before and after photos to really give an idea of how things will look once the strategy is executed. If you are looking at extending or redeveloping a

property get a good set of architectural drawings to show how the finished product will look.

You need to tell your investors how much they will pay for the property, your fees and any other costs you can predict up front. Make sure you demonstrate your value in the process by highlighting the level of discount from asking price, or opportunities you have found to add value. You can even look at having a valuation and appraisal done by a recognised valuation company to provide confidence to your clients.

In outlining the strategy you need to walk investors through the process. If your clients are not property professionals assume a limited knowledge base and avoid jargon. When you initially present the deal, less is more, but have the detail ready when they ask questions.

Make a note of what is included in your services, for example:

Finder's fee

Project coordination
Referral to builder / lettings agent / solicitor

Also make a note of services provided by third parties like:

Building work
Legal work
Valuations
Lettings services

It is important you don't try to do everything yourself. We are looking to build a business rather than a job in the first place, but you also need to be mindful that some aspects of property investing are for skilled professionals. For example, a builder is an expert at building and has insurance for when something goes wrong to cover himself or herself and the client, so you want the contract to be between the builder and the investor client buying the property so that the investor client is covered. Further, consider something unforseen does happen during a refurbishment and there is an extra £1,000 bill. If it is truly unforseen then that extra bill is a direct discussion between the builder and the client. You might help in the negotiation of cost, but your business would not pay the cost.

When you present your deals, keep your initial offering to 1 page, 2 pages at the maximum. The first time you show a client a deal, it is a sales pitch, so include the key information, how much will it cost, how much can they make? Always have detail prepared, if the client is genuinely interested he will quickly ask detailed questions and then you must have a detailed business plan or appraisal ready to go with supporting information. If you are referencing third party services in deals that you are selling onto your clients, include quotes and information from professional third parties on their letterhead.

CHAPTER SEVEN

POWER TEAM

As a property investor you need a power team to help you execute deals successfully. As a sourcing business you need a power team to help you both to run your business, but also to provide services to your clients that you can't provide in-house. In this chapter we look at some of the standard members to a sourcing agent's power team.

Property Valuer

Most property investors use finance to purchase property, and a key aspect of all finance is a valuation. By having a valuer as part of your team you have someone who is experienced and expert in their field who can provide the same valuation service a bank would expect before they would lend against a property. This is important for demonstrating your value in negotiating a great deal, in building trust with your clients, and also in being sure about the exit strategy for the property. Try to pick a valuer or valuation company that values to the same methodology or is on the panel for likely lenders for the property to minimise risk in the deal.

Solicitor

If you are dealing with an experienced investor they may have a solicitor they use regularly, but don't assume all your clients will. Find a good solicitor that you have a strong working relationship with that you feel comfortable referring clients to. Having a good relationship with a solicitor can speed up many complicated transactions and make them seem easy.

Builder

If you are sourcing properties that require any type of repair or refurbishment through to redevelopment, you will need a builder that is matched to the level of work required. On larger projects with significant sums of money involved you may want to get multiple quotes, or put the work out to tender to get the best price. On smaller jobs, a tried and trusted builder is an important member of your power team. If you are providing a builder with regular work, then the builder should provide a better and more consistent service to you and to your clients.

Estate Agents

It's important to know who are the best lettings and sales agents in your area, although they may not necessarily be the agents you buy from. Look at the exit strategy for the deal that your investor client is doing and line up a trusted agent to sell or rent the property so that you as a sourcing agent can end your involvement and move onto the next fee.

Mortgage broker

As with solicitors, experienced investors you deal with may have their own broker they use regularly, but if not, make sure you have a trusted broker in your network. If you have a regular broker you use or refer clients to, that should streamline the financing process. The broker may not know all your clients in advance, but if they know the style of deals you source, they will have a shortcut to the most likely lenders for those deals.

Insurance Broker

Streamline the process for your investors, as their exchange day is coming closer; be ready to refer them to your insurance broker. Many insurance brokers offer special rates for referred business, which is good news for your clients, and some pay referral fees as well which can go back to your profit margin.

Beyond the basic list, think about who else you

might need that is specific to the types of deals you find in your area. If you find many HMO opportunities, you may want to spend time networking with the environmental health team so you have a direct line for licensing queries. If you find development opportunities or lots of properties that would benefit from extension or change of use, then find a good local architect and planning consultant who can streamline your process for you and deliver outstanding service to your clients.

CHAPTER EIGHT

TAKING CARE OF BUSINESS

Like any other business, running a sourcing business starts with getting your business setup correctly. It's important to think about the structure of your business at the start, how you want to present your business and what will protect your business.

Structures

You have a choice of operating as a sole trader, partnership, limited liability partnership or as a limited company. From a practical point of view, none of the structures makes a lot of difference to the function of your business, but it does make a difference to your tax position and also to your liability in the event something does go wrong.

The size and scale of your business, or your business goals, may define what the best structure is for you from a tax perspective and you should speak with your accountant about your projected income, expenditure and turnover at the outset to plan what will be the best structure. It's important to have a detailed discussion with an accountant who knows your full financial picture to make sure that you're setup in the most efficient way from the start.

When thinking about structure you may also want to think about how you position your business. Some people feel their business has more weight if it is a limited company rather than a sole trader or partnership structure, so consider from a marketing and branding perspective. Equally you may prefer your customers to feel they are getting a personal 1 on 1 service, so you want your business to be a sole trader or partnership structure where there is very direct and personal contact to your client base.

You should also consider the liability and asset protection angle to your business at the outset. Consult with your solicitor to look at the pros and cons of your structure. Solicitors are paid to think about 'when' something goes wrong, not 'if' and to plan for your worst case scenario, so take that information on board. Consider, if someone brought legal action against you or your company what protections do the different operating structures offer?

Legal considerations

You should take legal advice early to set up and protect your business. Meet with your solicitor to talk through how the business will operate, what services you will offer, to whom and under what terms. It's very important that you create terms of business before you start taking fees. Terms of business should set out what you are taking a fee for, what services you guarantee and what services you don't guarantee. A quick example:

You present a deal that is 25% below market value.
The property has been valued today at £100,000 and you negotiate a discount to £75,000.
Your investor client buys the property on the basis of this information.
The investor client refinances the property after 6 months and the bank values the property at £92,000.
Nothing has physically changed with the property, but the market in that area has softened.
The investor comes to you seeking compensation as they believe they have lost £8,000 in value.

In the real world we know that investments can go up and down in value, and in an example like this, the market could change in that area next year and the property could be valued at £110,000. The investor must take the risk to enjoy the reward. However, from a legal point, it needs to be clear in your terms of business that you don't guarantee things like future value of the property. Think about all the things in any property deal that are outside your control. As a sourcing business it needs to be clear you are providing information to assist the investor in taking the educated risk, but it is their risk to take, not your business' risk to guarantee.

Managing deals and investors

You need to have a solid business process to deal with leads that come in so that you can turn them into deals, and then sell those deals onto your investors. Think carefully about the steps involved in executing the deal and create a management plan. Many sourcing businesses create a database to track information on leads and deals.

Consider the scale of your business when setting up your systems, if you are just starting your business you may be the negotiator, secretary, deal manager, accounts manager and book-keeper all in one. However, as your business grows, identify solutions to bring people into your business. Your sourcing business profits when you can find and sell deals, so outsource tasks that enable you to do the things that really make you money.

CHAPTER NINE

REGULATION

Regulation and compliance can have a negative connotation. For a professional sourcing agent though, showing you are properly registered and complying with all relevant legislation should build your prestige and build trust with your client base.

Sourcing agents and sourcing businesses fall under the same regulatory umbrella as estate agents. In the Estate Agents Act 1979, estate agency work is defined as:

- introducing and/ or negotiating with people who want to buy or sell freehold or leasehold

property (or their Scottish equivalents) including commercial or agricultural property
- where this is done in the course of a business
- pursuant to instructions from a client

You can read the full legislation online at www.legislation.gov.uk/ukpga/1979/38.

If your work or your business's work does fall under the definition of Estate Agency under the act then you must be registered with the Office of Fair Trading.

The Estate Agents Redress Act 2007 requires all persons or companies undertaking estate agency work as defined by the Estate Agents Act 1979 to be registered with The Property Ombudsman.

You can read more about this legislation online at www.legislation.gov.uk/ukpga/2007/17/contents.

In the market place there is a difference between

an estate agent who acts for sellers of properties, and the sourcing agent who acts on behalf of buyers, but the legislation treats both the same.

In practical terms this means that a sourcing business needs to comply with the legislation. The key compliance items that you need to be aware of are:

Registration with the Office of Fair Trading
Registration with the Property Ombudsman
Consider registration with the Information Commissioners Office.
Registration with the OFT

You must be registered with the Office of Fair Trading as an estate agent for anti-money laundering. Guidance on this can be obtained on the OFT's website at www.oft.gov.uk/OFTwork/estate-agents/#.Ut_Ph6U4m_t. There are detailed guides produced by the OFT in terms of meeting your compliance requirements, however in laymen's terms your requirements as a sourcing business are:

To verify the identity of the clients you are dealing with

- If you are introducing the buyer and seller then you need to have identified both using documents like passports and utility bills to verify both their identity and their address
- You must keep this information on file
- The OFT can ask to inspect your file of information at any time

To verify the source of funds for clients you are dealing with

- You need to establish the person agreeing to purchase the property has the means to do so i.e. cash/savings/a mortgage offer
- You need to take reasonable steps to see how the money was built up i.e. saved, sale of another property or investment

There is a degree of common sense to meeting your compliance requirements with the OFT. If you have

A PROPERTY SOURCING BUSINESS

a client who earns minimum wage as a cleaner showing you £1,000,000 in the bank to invest, alarm bells should be ringing vs a client who is a Doctor earning £100,000 salary with a £50,000 deposit saved. If in doubt, speak to your solicitor about what sort of information you need to collect and keep on file.

Note that when you register with the OFT some details will be published publicly about the person and company registering.

Registration with The Property Ombudsman

To register with The Property Ombudsman you must supply details of your business and your activities in regards to estate agency work. This can be done online and information is available at this website: www.tpos.co.uk. One of the key requirements is that you have adequate insurance cover to indemnify your clients if they make a loss as a result of your negligence (as an individual or a company). You should look at adequate business insurance before you begin registration with the OFT.

Do you need to register with the Information Commissioners Office?

Any company, which holds personal details, may have a requirement to be registered with the ICO. In general, the majority of estate agency work does require registration, so that means that a sourcing business would need to be registered.

On the Information Commissioners Office website there are a number of guides to personal information that you can review. More importantly though, there is an online checklist which will look at your business activity and let you know whether you do need to be registered or not. You can find more information here: http://ico.org.uk.

There is a charge to be registered with the bodies noted above. It is worth noting the charges for registration, and any ongoing fees, are very minimal when contrasted with the fines for non-compliance.

CHAPTER TEN

CASE STUDY – ARDEN HANLEY INVESTOR AND SOURCING AGENT

'Sourcing property is a fantastic complimentary business to property investing. It helped me supercharge my own strategy from buying a property every 6 months to buying 1 a month' says investor and sourcing agent Arden Hanley.

Arden's sourcing business grew organically from his investment activities.

'When I first started as a property investor, I was focused on purchasing distressed properties that could be refurbished into buy to lets. Using a forced appreciation strategy I was able to recycle capital from the purchase of the first property to use for the acquisition of the next, however, given the six month rule from mortgage lenders it was slow going.'

Arden found very quickly that because lending rules required that he bought and held a property for a minimum of 6 months before refinancing it, he was passing up many good investment opportunities because of a lack of funds available at the time. Setting up a sourcing business was a very natural complimentary business to start early on as a way of monetising the deals left on the table and building his investment capital.

'Sourcing properties had a number of benefits for me. First, I started to build up my capital pot with the fees generated allowing me to enter multiple deals at once. I found that the deals I was being offered through estate agents started becoming more attractive, as they could see that either through myself or through my sourcing business I was providing a good volume of business for them.'

Arden benefited from increased volume of work for his power team as well. By having larger turnover and a standard specification, refurbishment costs and times went down.

'Looking at my average refurbishment cost from year 1 where I did minimal sourcing, to year 2 where I was sourcing quite a lot of property for people, I can see a huge discount on materials cost – about 25%. Most of this discount was down to either the builder, or in some cases me directly doing enough business on a trade account to get a better price. As most of what I was sourcing on required refurbishment as well as that being my personal investment strategy, I got good turnover incentives. The builder's labour costs didn't drop dramatically, but I suddenly found I could always get a tradesperson for a late night repair call-out as I was funnelling the team a lot of business.'

Reduced refurbishment cost increased margin on a

number of the deals Arden did for himself, but also gave his sourcing business a competitive edge as they could negotiate better refurbishment prices on behalf of clients. Similarly to the building works side, letting management costs also went down due to the volume he was bringing into the agents.

'Because I was referring all my sourcing business clients to the same lettings agency that was managing my properties, we quickly started enjoying 2-3% discount on full management fees. That doesn't seem like a lot, but when you spread that across a bunch of properties each month you start to see a lot more cash in the bank at the end of the year.'

When Arden started sourcing, his business was focused on similar deals to what he was finding for himself, distressed buy to let opportunities or flip opportunities. As his confidence as an investor grew, he also started looking at larger projects to source onto other investors.

'My sourcing business has always been complimentary to my investing activities, so as I scaled up into HMO and small flat developments, I realised I had the systems in place to do those deals, so I could also sell those opportunities to others. The great thing about doing that is that my average fees have now gone up significantly, but the volume of deals I'm a part of has reduced.'

Arden has some tips for those starting out in the sourcing business:

'Don't present deals you wouldn't do yourself if you had the resources. It's important for your clients to trust you – it's much easier to earn a fee from a retained client than keep on getting new ones. If you create a good strategy for a property and there's margin in it then you can name your price – I tend to price according to work involved and headroom in the deal rather than property value. Most importantly don't sell yourself short – if you've invested in educating yourself in property, charge appropriately for that knowledge.'

Arden deals with a very small client base, preferring to do larger projects with larger fees for a smaller number of clients.

'This has always been a side business, rather than a focus so I want to make sure I get good return on my time invested. I know other people in the sourcing business who focus solely on this as their strategy though, and it's an easy business to generate £5,000-£10,000 a month from if you set up your systems right and put a good power team around you. The key is to put your systems together well from the start, that's where your training and education helps – you're already 10 steps ahead of anyone else.'

CHAPTER ELEVEN

CASE STUDY

Making money from sourcing property is all about leveraging your specialist knowledge, and staying in the middle of the deal. Being in the middle is more important than owning the deal for the sourcing agent. As the example below shows, doing your research on a deal and knowing where to look can make you money as the sourcing agent and your investors a healthy profit too, everybody wins.

The twice sourced property:

The property was a large corner building in the student area of Nottingham.

Listed for sale with a local agent as a large house for sale at £140,000. At the time Nottingham had recently brought in an article 4 restriction limiting permitted conversion of family houses to HMOs. While this property was in a student area, the estate agent marketing the property did not believe it could be let to students because of the article 4. They were wrong. The property was owned by a post-grad student who had been letting out 3 other bedrooms to his mates to subsidise his mortgage during his degree, so the property had established and continuing use as a HMO prior to the article 4. Here's how the numbers stacked up the first time the property was sourced onto an investor, Investor 1.

Asking price: £140,000
Current rents: £260 x 3 rooms (No HMO License & Mates rates)
Negotiated purchase price: £135,000
Open market room rate: £300-£325 per month per room = £1,875 per month gross
(3 x small rooms, 3 x large rooms)

Refurbishment required: £2,000
(Minor redecoration and the cost of a HMO license)
Sourcing Fee: £7,000
Legal Fees: £2,000
Total Investor 1 Outlay: £146,000

The refurbishment budget on this was very low, as it had been done to HMO standards. Luckily for the purchaser of the property, the previous owner had considered turning it into a fully fledged HMO at one point in the past and had put in fire alarm systems and fire doors, and then decided he didn't want that many housemates.

Investor 1 bought the property in late 2012, paying a £7,000 sourcing fee. The property was initially purchased by Investor 1 with a 65% interest only mortgage, a HMO license was obtained and then tenants were put into the property, which made the numbers for Investor 1 look like this:

Gross rents:
£1,875 per month

 A PROPERTY SOURCING BUSINESS

(Based on 6 rooms let for the academic year)
Allow 35% for costs £656.25
(HMO running costs, bills for services,
lettings management, maintenance etc)
Mortgage payments @ 6% £438.75
Net cash flow to the investor £780

However Investor 1's strategy wasn't buy and hold, he was looking for a chunk of money. So he came back to the sourcing company to ask if anyone was looking for a ready made investment with leases in place. The property was marketed through a sourcing agent in May 2013.

Value as a fully let student HMO: £200,000

Available for: £155,000

Gross Rents: £1,875 per month
(Pre let for 2013/2014 from September 1st to July 31st)

Sourcing Fee: £10,000

Investor 2 Legal Costs: £1,000

Investor 2 purchased the property and paid the sourcing fee on August 1st, 1 month before first rents were due in for the pre-let tenants. So Investor 1 made the following profit:

9 month's rental profit at £780 per month: £7,020

Profit on flip: £9,000

Total profit for Investor 1: £16,020

Investor 2 had a complete armchair investment setup with leases in place.

Investor 2's outlay: £166,000

Equity Profit based on £200,000 value: £34,000

Gross rents: £1,875 per month
(Based on 6 rooms let for the academic year)

Allow 35% for costs: £656.25
(HMO running costs, bills for services, lettings management, maintenance etc)

Mortgage payments @ 6%: £700
Based on 70% loan on full value

Net cash flow to the investor: £518.75

Residual cash in the deal: £26,000

Investor 2 makes a healthy cash flow each year and a 24% return on their money which is not bad for someone who works for an IT company and to quote, 'doesn't really understand how property works.' Investor 1 makes £16,020 for holding an asset for 10 months. The sourcing agent, who hasn't had to outlay to purchase the property, or had a Capital Gains Tax bill on sale, has managed to make £17,000 staying in the middle of the transaction.

CHAPTER TWELVE

CONCLUSION

This introduction to the sourcing business is designed to help the investor see the potential of creating a business through controlling and negotiating deals and earning a fee from that work. The key to successfully running a sourcing business is finding good opportunities and seeing potential where other people don't, that's how you make yourself valuable to investor clients and ensure they keep coming back for your expert service. Whether you use this as a primary strategy to be in the middle of the deal without having to outlay the money yourself, or it becomes a secondary strategy for the deals you don't want, the earning potential

 A PROPERTY SOURCING BUSINESS

is clear. We wish you the very best of luck on your Brick Buy Brick journey.

This book is part of the Brick Buy Brick series, created in association with Tigrent Learning UK Ltd, who have been at the forefront of UK investment training since 2002.

Copyright ©2014 Tigrent Learning UK Limited

www.brick-buy-brick.co.uk

BRICK BUY BRICK A PROPERTY SOURCING BUSINESS

NOTES

NOTES

BRICK BUY BRICK A PROPERTY SOURCING BUSINESS

NOTES

NOTES

NOTES

NOTES